6

# The Memory of the Drift

**Also by Paul Holman**

The Fabulist (1991)
The Memory of the Drift, Book 1 (2001)

*for Louise
with love

Paul
21/7/2012*

# PAUL HOLMAN

# The Memory of the Drift

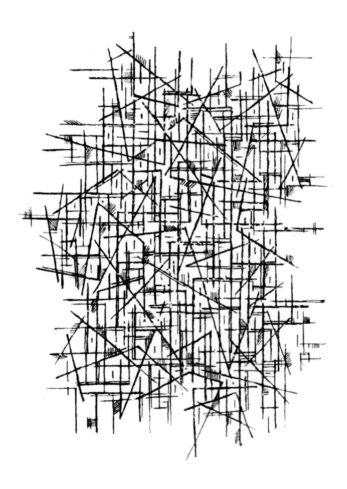

**Shearsman Books**
Exeter

Published in the United Kingdom in 2007 by
Shearsman Books Ltd
58 Velwell Road
Exeter EX4 4LD          www.shearsman.com

ISBN-13  978-1-905700-29-5

ISBN-10  1-905700-29-6

Acknowledgements
An earlier version of 'The Genii of a Secret State' was published as *The Memory of the Drift*, Invisible Books, 2001.

'In the Common Era', 'Dog Mercury' and 'Vicinal' have all been published online, in successive versions, by Peter Philpott at *Great Works*: he has my deepest gratitude for his patience and involvement with this project.

Some of the texts in this book were conceived as Field Study Emanations and have been published as such in the *Journal of Field Study International* from year to year. Others have appeared in the following publications: *Abramelin* (online), *Angel Exhaust* (including 2 issues republished online at pinko.org and the Poetry Library website), *CCCP 13 Review*, *Haiku Quarterly*, *Lost & Found Times*, *Mindbaum*, *Poetry Salzburg Review*, *Ramraid Extraordinaire*, *Silver Star* (online) and *West Coast Line*. My thanks to their editors – some friends, some unknown to me.

The previous edition of *The Memory of the Drift* was dedicated to Ian Hamilton Finlay: both the affection and the consciousness of debt which that implies still hold in his absence.

The publisher gratefully acknowledges financial assistance from Arts Council England.

# Contents

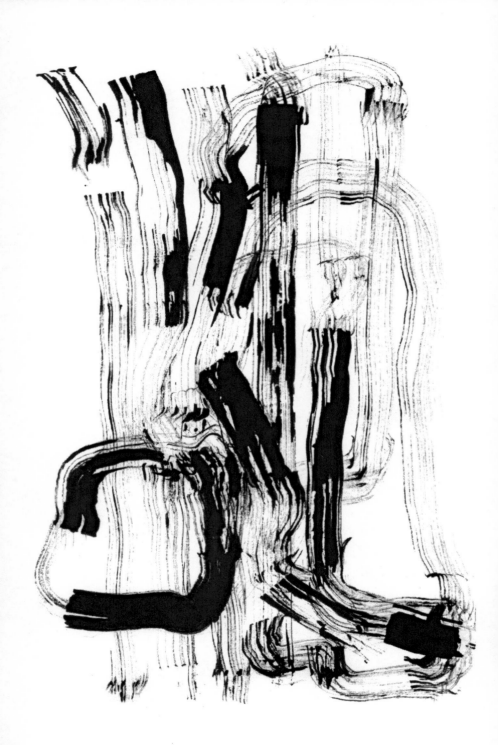

# The Memory of the Drift

# The Genii of a Secret State

He selected the great
closed helmet: it
might have fitted god
or hobgoblin. The
borrowed tape of star
music pleased him:
his trumpet of Helium

2

This blur of angels:
     the trace
of a more brilliant
language. Some
diminish into cloud,
     too rapid
[     ] birds' flicker
[           ]
find a common shape
     in flower,
star, Medusa's head:
their sign. It
shed that precision
     [     ] us
no first loved site,
no haunt [   ]
their note on space
     must fade
[                    ]
[         ] leave
these altered folds,
     turn wild
among hart's tongue
or catnip. The
ghost we dismantled
     is silent:
even the underworld
fails us. Each
masque of shepherds
     [        ]
that looked trivial
once [        ]

3

        I
      were roads
   upon which
     one
       sleek
   monster
    of
     but
  the true
    of

   I believed
there were roads
  upon which
    one might meet
not the sleek
   monster
    of some child's
story, but
   the true carrier
    of flames

4

My course is serpentine:
even the rich field
that I made too little
of, still held
back by the austerity
of my childhood's
eye, was never clear
but phantasmal

5

their code of romance
each lover forced
upon that sacred blue
note the dragon's
how some who received
into London. Even
enough to be a medium
powerful I raised

their code of romance
fail. The kindest
are led into the trap:
each lover forced
to select noose, mesh
or leash. I tread
upon that sacred blue
still to be found
beneath stem and barb,
note the dragon's
path. It is no longer
dangerous to tell
how some who received
the divine signal
sent their hooks down
into London. Even
to number them turned
me stupid, docile
enough to be a medium
for their angelic
discoveries. The most
powerful I raised
coughed fire, circled
reeking furniture

**6**

or kill the oppressive lie
to destruction. I set
[                              ]
[                  ] her face
on her world is accidental:
with liberty [          ]
immune to the satisfaction

to release her unhappiness
aside from experience
of both to let fascination
a decade since I last
[          ] possess a temper
a companion to desire:
by a newly deserved recoil
but do not ever spell

is curious and indifferent
[                              ]
and prefer to keep nothing
to gain love. My hold
how demonic I might become
of an alien [          ]
how I split the text apart

or kill the oppressive lie
that I might help her:
to release her unhappiness
into a regulated life
is curious and indifferent
to destruction. I set
her scar and her split lip
aside from experience
to turn upon a starry axis
[                              ]
[                                  ]

count it too wasteful
of both to let fascination
dissolve a friendship
and prefer to keep nothing
[          ] her face
become labelled and secret
a decade since I last
practiced such crude magic
to gain love. My hold
on her world is accidental:
an absence of control
[        ] possess a temper
uneven enough to show
how demonic I might become
with liberty [        ]
but restraint is no longer
a companion to desire:
it is shrouded in the home
of an alien [        ]
immune to the satisfaction
of being less haunted
by a newly deserved recoil
[        ] to consider
how I split the text apart

to make space for her name
but do not ever spell
it in full [              ]

7

absent | vacant | | erase | dissolve | | vanish

8: *Herdsman*

too severe to accept
some woodland
king for his model.
In delirium
the yellow waste
bag became an animal
and delicate red
bird life crackled
in the harsh
air of the isolation
ward. Of course I
am no better than
a declassé market
trader. Horus:
*This wine is corked*

9: *Stargazer*

fucked up. In 1979 I
had no idea
that Pam Burnel
was a name
used by Allen
Fisher. He counted
the letter K
three times in the design
on my cigarette
packet. The blast
must have damaged
that witches' launch
pad on the Isle
of Dogs. Each leaf
game that my daughter
invented

## 10: *Het Up*

the alcohol behind each chocolate
| sketch: eye | more beautiful
in this migraine glitter. I tell
her that the Greenwich axeman
is a sad | scribble | hair fixed
in a chopstick halo no weirder
than a biro or two. That smashed
cat head is just wood | space |
painted some kind of elfin hunt
upon the second

11: *Sally Day*

it is shrouded | hood |
but the other siren
is kind | haze hedge |
taught me to construct
a bomb: match
head and nail varnish
| deluge | bird catcher |
her crayon spectre upon
the blackboard

## 12: *Urusei Yatsura*

but element is less useful
to her than the correct armour
| how she followed
a life that coiled overhead
to dock in cloud |
did not mean to hold her emblem
in the supernatural world

13: *Nomiya Maki*

1

her

blue
in

lens

2

her
eye
behind
the
blue
square
set
in
a
clear
round
lens

14: *Skrimsl*

the most for
sending us that
Pizzicato Five tape
Erica bought a
second golf
       ball
bulb for our
spinning ghost and
moon lamp on
Roman but used
Albers
      as his
Pantone book odd
to have a
childhood in which
Hugues Cuenod figured

15: *The Sunken House*

he spoke of
Combat 18 in
a whisper just
that man with
long hair
       not
me his friend
the white Muslim
Halloween ghost over
a cardboard cross
read
     that mask
of terror as
some field where
a rabbit or
thirteen might assemble

16: *Erl*

1

left
on
indicate
the
the
the
fluorescent
pavement
tunnel's
rune
to
course

2

left the fluorescent rune on the
pavement to indicate the
tunnel's course

17: *Nettle*

found herself a ghost
world | crimson
silhouette of a bird |
paper bag monster
head | wand | turned
back into hail on the
kitchen floor

18

          the alcohol
          behind
               each chocolate

     sketch: eye

more beautiful
          in this migraine
     glitter. I tell
          her that the Greenwich
          axeman
     is a sad

                    scribble

     hair fixed
          in a chopstick halo
          no weirder
               than a biro
               or two. That smashed
               cat head
               is just wood

space

          painted
               some kind
          of elfin
                    hunt
          upon the second

19

but cast revolution
into neoplatonism made
stupid. I have
named texts after
two different brands
of fuse

my clothes
singed by Faust's
blowtorch. In 1989
I could think
of nothing but
nature over again
after Lovecraft. I
sleep beside the
red sister of
Jill Bioskop each

Mark E
Smith took the
spread fingers of
Wyndham Lewis for
his stencil. She
told me of

damage to herself
that I'd heard
described as fated.


indefinite

20

the route home
from the underworld
is marked
by two feathers  crossed
on the pavement
the clear
plastic tube
from a bicycle
lock  a cigarette
packet and a drift
of spilled
matches  a bus
ticket and another
feather

21: *Eurasian*

in various
forms of
mask and
silence the
spiral I'd
looked for
around the
neck of
a dancer
more red
tangled on
a kind
of nomad


    not
formed a
fool   R
okuro-Kub
i   made
shadow an
insect
a halluc
ination *a*
*ll* shared
is not


the hut
of fog in
  could
imitation
I of
to guard

against
this letter
but
asked for
control
of

22

but their action had damaged
the future also Sun Ra correct
to hold Pharaoh above Moses
beautiful an architecture of
some being of dragon temple
most unable to support a
forested west did not intend
to feed the mermaid estranged boat
builders' wood is a ghost
ride the office named Ragnarok
still vacant


identified the tattoo as her
mermaid rubber stamp had once
been a knuckle girl in rust
on Hazel's tinsel badge found
that I'd pushed the baby cart
into a gun siege hand
moth no longer settled on styled
himself prince of the dragon
tract through which a girl
in the Ohmu eye of a broken
Hotpoint Heldscalla the
negative of the Odradek Stadium


Henry James would have cared
for the delicate cut the great
still lizard in a dreamed
encounter to haunt the eye
trapped behind honeycomb or
lightning the blood bought disgust
me

23

tell Mas Abe no
seam our dog
buried upright
at the orchard
gate image head
mover head of
the blue star on
broken metal

24: *Indifferent*

night cough is
                    lightning
draft

          marked
                    with peppermint
cigarette
          held

                    in a

splinted hand each

                              high
small breast
                    and her

navel
          made that me

intermingled

                    no glass
                              coffin

after a

          car crash
in
     but not

                    of

the straight cloud
                              held

a dog
         neither mercury
nor

         platinum mesh stretched

above the

              hospital
                        of
both her
         stone

                        deterioration
compared
              to that shimmer

**25:** *Naivling*

the printer
Arb
    er part
of

  a

     ma
       rke
t traders'
c
  ortège int
erpre
    ted

     Ov
id as

    *Cap*
     *it*
*al* of Chine
se

  blood in
a

  cam
    oufla
ge shirt

m

    o

st belong t

o t

  he


    schoo

l

  of sk

    ull

on a stick

26

I find government
in the
     wood
moth whir and
blue
    halo

       uprising
but of that

no football in
the shop
      most
unable

    to support
a
  forested
west ideology
economy ideology

in shit on

      the
wall
   of the
commune a hut
       boy
prophet mounted
by

   the
     skeleton
handful of

hard white
              wood
   a hand of bone

27

not the open


hand
         but
    the


    circuit

    of


course
enlightenment

is


    the same

    thing


         as
order

Ben and Esther

big

character

poster
        in

sleep the

least

destructive
is
        handed

a weapon

## 28: *Elflock*

hours clouds
        ghosts




merge
    bone
        hand
forced



      against the

blue



   hinge
      of
all
  those



    I



glimpsed in the

muster

        circled once

blew

    fire
      wet
stinking

        rink lagoon

his

    shirt

      had
the
    same boring

image of

       riot
his
   bag


     an
alien
    head logo

## In the Common Era

*29: Headless*

I am the shadow
of a man

who is not
demonic, who
might well
be kind,
          too
straightforward,
no
    less
irresolute
and
        harried
than I am.

But I
      value
her limitlessness,

her
instability:
I
  would not
care to drag
her
      back. I
am frightened

that I
might not notice

if she lost
herself.

LOUISE: I dream that I get shot.

PAUL: Does the dream continue after you are dead?

LOUISE: No. I have a method to end it. I can leave any nightmare if I recite a nursery rhyme: *Baa baa black sheep* . . .

PAUL: I dreamed that Death stood next to me at an exhibition of primitive art. I recognised him because of the earth on his coat and his musty smell.

I had caught sight of him once before: then he stood in the stairwell of an apartment block. He carried a pad of lined paper and a pen.

He arranged letters taken from his name in a fresh order: this operation created a different name. He wrote each new name upon a sheet of paper: he then detached the sheet from the pad and folded it across.

He stood in front of my living room window. I could not look directly at his face. I heard the letterbox rattle: he had posted a sheet of notepaper through it.

My friend rose to open the door.

LOUISE: I used to dream that my father stood behind me and held me. He would be gentle at first: then his grip became painful.

I turned and looked at an evil creature: it was identical to my father.

## 31: *Falsified*

### 1

In childhood I had encountered Yaldebaoth: an emission of sleet. The shale contained the image of a god: head and torso of silver flecked blue, elongated eye, bulbous beak which tapered to an arrowhead, beige stump of a wing.

### 2

I felt that he put me down because I dealt in the manner of a Jew. He held my hand to be less clean than one forced to bring drink or food to his sort. It did me no good to resent the hoard that had been condensed into his craftsmanship.

### 3

Her life had become too scattered to collect. Even spite failed to assemble a coherent figure from such material. There must have been little choice but to damage all that had been made for herself. I did not pretend to contain her: at once woodland and mermaid eyed.

### 4

I considered her to be a sort of prophetess. She might raise her voice or dance in silence. The lit red room and open market merged for her. Once she confronted me on my route home from the shop: both smiled when I met her adrift in her nightdress on the pavement.

### 5

Of course she had guessed that I contained the abyss. There was nothing for me to do but clutch at her as though I meant to hurl her aside. I knew that her dialectic would reveal me to be hideous and worn out. In the end I made desolate the friendship that could not be transformed.

## 6

I tried to begin my mission among the dead. The angel beside me let my skin unravel: bone dropped from bone where I stood. It did no good that she withheld herself. Still I turned upon her. Fuck it. Fuck it. I did not follow my nature.

32

Debonair Midas, do
not even consider
the form I
have settled into:
it made failure
radiant blue, foreign
to that sealed
moment in nothing
to do.


        Marginalia:
I edited the
torn-off stub of
clouds and great
stars, thunders and
folds of air.

33: *La Montagne*

How I fail to measure
an intensity
not directed toward
me: a magical operation.
So take him, in spite
of friendship

and revolutionary
biography. A critique of
nature in the name of
Prometheus:
white gigantic phantoms
of granite reptiles and
animals.

      The force
that drags the
operator upright is
a means of liberation. I
never understood that
I had been
incompetent, stupid,

often a burning nail,
diabolic. Too difficult
to capture this
suspension of feeling
or the ghostly pain of
my double.

34

1

Dejection of the archangel in London: I
drop hair, clothes of paper, all paper.

2

No monotonous cloud, no figure of folds,
but residence of the spirit in language.

## 35: My Negative Freedom

I think of a woman who was not in fact my mother carefully peeling and slicing an apple for herself with a small wooden handled knife. In the course of a succession of days in which neither of us had the imagination to escape from a house not so very deep in the country, she would talk of her marriage and of torture inflicted upon her by her own mother in some utopian estate at the edge of London.

(When she had been ash for a dozen years I found myself in love with a girl who brought the sense of her upbringing back to me: she would return from a visit to her mother with a black eye or split lip, fingermarks purple on each arm.)

The matter least discussed was that of my origin. My entire knowledge of this had been drawn from a single intense glimpse of a forbidden document. I had been left with the belief that human relationship was a possession granted through language.

She made a ritual of lighting a cigarette or breaking a bar of chocolate in the manner of a person who had nothing to spare. The realisation that she had such a poor life, that she could be at once so vivid and so desperately insubstantial was my first experience of the process of tearing aside the world with which I was familiar that I would learn to call dialectic.

More or less everything she told me was wrong. Whether she meant to or not, she taught me that the only defence against entrapment was to reduce experience to a narrative and then pray that the event itself might become forgotten. (I find the most honest course is to learn to be inarticulate, never so much as write a letter.)

## 36

Still I kept my faith
in the dream-criticism
for which I had
neglected all that
the daylit world first
offered: it took
no gift to foretell
that the order I
believed to exercise
power in secret must
accomplish nothing. I
let myself be consumed
while I slept to
dedicate a path to
the promiscuous ghost
which had inhabited
me for a season: it
remained the kindest
that might be drawn
from underground given
my well-known hatred
of attachment.

37

Even with my head slung
from its leash of hair I
did not follow the path
back to the green chapel.

It proved all too difficult
to negate the claim that
I had just risen from
the bed of a demoniac.

No doubt I might borrow
the outfit of a goblin priest
and summon foul luck
for the sake of a poem.

I had little prospect but
to review my old ambition
of being a comrade to
the aimless or vagabond.

38

I asked to be mistaken
for some phantom of the
paper world. No wonder
that I slipped through so
much of the routine of
exchange and possession.

# Dog Mercury

39

so Canidia drew on

a spell of fog (dry cloud)

the moulting cage

cat shit in the wickerwork

40

My devilish friend,
I heard of
one who settled
upon the flood
plain as comrade
to a grandson
of the siren –
all hedges stiff
with dried mud
from the river:
this great princess
rejected the gospel –
a shrine to
the dog star,
a cat ruled
the star mice –
her throat encircled
by amber, by
jet. She laughed
to find a
thread of my
sperm upon the
garment of nettles:
her grave ornaments
of chalk beside
the shepherd's crown.

41

1

Hawk moth fetched a rumour of the sensuous external world: the path
of Diana climbed from Tiphareth into the abyss.

2

In December we kept each other company through the hermetic
wilderness, kissed while the moon stood at the pillar of mercy.

3

Myself a half-apparent man, I found her pronouncements clouded: it
had become habitual for her to gaze through a net.

4

I forgot those who knew me best, spent too much thought upon a ghost
I had embraced among blossoms of salt and sulphur.

5

The blackberry stain inside my hat, its brim twisted into a figure of
eight for the sake of contrast to her curious star-pointed halo.

6

Morgan le Fay gathered strength through the Bronze Age: no longer
bound to the sky, her genius settled deep within spring and pool.

7

Under the cloud barrier, we passed black sheds of the giants, the
paddock in which fairground equipment stood dismantled.

**8**

My conceit outlasted art, trade and mystery: the damaged launch in drydock upon a wooded peninsula, bridge knotted into the fist of some freshwater god.

**9**

How foolish of me to hold that I stood back from one who might well not have been taken, more keen to enact an old refusal than to become subject to happiness.

**10**

The demands and menaces of poets had ceased to impress me long ago: I wished only to sit down and put my back to a tree.

**11**

I made nothing of the secret breathed to me in syllables, still Marxist, still Marxist under the rose.

**12**

Do not forget that many gods are buried within this island: our dead go elsewhere, in a boat steered by the thought of Mercury.

42

Though I stepped
once again between
those wyvern-guarded
gates, to follow each
path mown through a
delicate large meadow
where the bee orchid
grew, it was not
to encounter some-
body I had loved more
than any other, become
an omen of herself alone.

43

My companion had too
much sense to admit
a visitor to our
bed or dream that
we might perish together.
In donkey jacket and
silver raincoat we set
out upon a spiral
path which led from
London to the coast
and back to a
city which had taken
on the appearance of
a left handed drawing.
We made one wasteful
move after another out
of a timid restlessness
and the growing necessity
not to be traced.

44

Headless, I had been
defined as the most powerful
creature, no longer subject to
the witch flight of thought.
I knew myself to
be a sentence uttered by
the god, become ironic, spiteful
enough to consume all that
nature offered.

45

By the law of threefold
return, I committed myself
to a sidelong life,
my beard now white
at the chin. Isabel took
bone to dowse,
her cardigan fixed by a
safety pin across her breasts:
she might have stood with
the horned crown and sword at
her feet.

46

In the backyard
I make a comical enough
figure of the hermit,
storm lantern raised
between the washing
line and the rose on its
trellis.

My life defined by
adoption, each demon
that migraine generated,
my infatuation with
the motley-sandalled girl.

# Vicinal

*47: Faunus / Felix*

My co-walker
traced the lemniscus
around two black-
bird eggs my daughter's cat
had left out-
side the back door.

I did not share
his delight in clouds
and unemphatic asexual
nudity but sank
down into the mud earth:
wet, humid, stagnant, occult.

Too wayward to heed
the slow thought of metals,
I adopted the death posture . . .

48: *Soror Mystica*

Now she has turned
in the birchwood to
face the watchtower
of the east, her left
breast golden, the
right involved in
the drift of blue that
began around her eye
socket and extended
in a diagonal across
her belly, her arms
oddly unpainted from
the elbow down.

49: *To Madimi*

I had no intention of
being numbered among
the people of the book:
little more
than a child, I aligned
myself with the gods
and derided the household
as animal.

I tried to set down
the system that my angel
taught, but found her
code dead upon
paper: the transmission
faltered because of
some lack within myself,
the medium.

I wished to accomplish
a style that heaven or hell
might find lucid: from
the outset I
knew the limit of each
book and the configuration
of material it should
contain.

(It had been left up
to me to assemble such a
canon as best I could
from any text
that came to hand.)

I did not understand
how I might oppose a power
indifferent to its location

in culture:
there could be no
resistance but a willed
failure, the decision to leave
no archive.

50

I sneezed
in the slant
of sun, too
slow-witted
to answer
the riddle
set by this
champion of
a culture
expressed
in the ripple
of ancient
terraces,
the shallow
bowl of a
dew pond.

## 51

My friend
stood laugh
ing be
side the
crow trap.

52

I had no choice
but to undo the spell
which language had cast
upon me when, in
the days of autonomia,
I first met one by whom I
was to be consumed
and then made
afresh: she taught me
that an operation
performed upon the
tongue must transform
the world.

53: *The Shoulder Bite*

She taught me that
Diana stole in the form
of a cat to the bed
of her brother,
the Morning Star. *(He
dge ghost and so forth,
lifted upon the bree
ze.)* She taught
me to prefer the nomad
to the deracinated:
both inhabit a zone
between paradise
and liberation. *(Fra
gments of words I glimps
ed falling from the
revolving tower
in darkness and flam
e.)* How bourgeois, how
academic she had become:
I laughed to
think of how I had
descended among the
emarginati to seek her.

54

Not so long before, I
had dreamed of both
of us walking in between
those same trees
through which she led
me onto the common,
past a dead slow-worm
and tadpoles in their pool,
to find coral root
among the nettles.

## 55: *Adam Belial*

One sunset his mother led him to the landing window. She told him that the world must perish underneath just such a sky. Then the sun itself would flicker out.

The path he had been forced to walk led through an orchard to the refuse heap outside a farm cottage. In view of the black upper window of the cottage he turned over the ragged skull of a cow. He had been initiated into a system based upon decay and exhaustion.

Childhood had been his tomb. Most adults found him stupid or puzzling. One or two treated him as though they expected to find him in dispute at the temple.

He fell beneath the enchantment of one who taught him to make the life of the mind seamless with his experience of the world. For her there could be no distinction between the passion of Holger Meins and the use of her own sexuality.

At twilight he followed a trail of blood through the house to the corner in which his mother sat. She told him that she had fallen from a three-legged stool she had been standing upon. But it was not his father who spat at him or struck him in the face.

56

She had been earthed
(had I earthed
her by my intrusion?)
eyes no longer turned

upon phenomena I
could not locate.
She considered me a
plunderer, a fecund man,

a madman: one who
scries alphabets
of daggers, of arrows.
Zigzagged tights in a

knot in her pocket,
the tip of each
hair luminous as fox-
fire or rotten wood,

she opened the violet
gate at her throat
to release the fractal
silhouette of Pan.

57: *Zigzaggedness*

In the pub garden,
how I jumped at each clack
of that horse jaw!
I had defined
myself as some witch's
brat from the tale I
read long ago, intent
upon leaving no
record of my life,
but an absence that any
fool might occupy in
capricious play.
Find me by the dis-
placement I create: my
friends burnt in cages,
hanged or drowned
in shallow pools.
So much for the young
man who first walked
along the pink
roads of Lanarkshire,
under the gaze of the
buzzards in the wood,
to visit an idyll
conceived in anger.
Perhaps this or that
odd-looking girl
was my beloved:
eye paint to enable
clairvoyance, bead-net
dress over a sheath
dress, bead-net
dress with nipple cups.
A pallet sprinkled
with moth dust: by what
sympathetic magic

did one drop of
red show in the sperm in
the palm of the hand
open before me?
With thumb raised
to mouth, my ghost slid t
hrough drift, throug
h field, through
double current.
Even in pipistrelle light,
in summer, I hesitated
to enter that
labyrinth, in which
no game is forbidden.

58: *From a Magic Opera*

ASMODEUS: It is not true that she is passive, but she is unresponsive: a remark, a gift, a touch are gravely received and never returned. It is part of her real forbearance: I have benefited from it often enough.

SARAH: The demon that once walked beside me has made a new home in each hand: instead of the roar and flicker that I could never purge from my head, I am tormented by the sensation of each wrist melding into an immobile wedge of bone.

ASMODEUS: Even though I do not receive acknowledgement from her, I am not turned away: she will not let me test the limit of her toleration before the act. I occupy her silence with a greater commitment than I had intended.

SARAH: I could distinguish no form but the angel and the skeleton: even I found it too characteristic that I believed them to exist in parallel. I could never accept this angel sheathed in bone or a skeleton that meat and shit had encrusted.

ASMODEUS: The fact that she has refused me nothing has made me cautious: I am afraid that I might commit an irrevocable error. Her friends belong to separate parts of her life: her origin is definitive, her allegiance peripheral.

59

From the bus I
gazed at the corrugated
iron walls of the hut near
the airfield in
which the redeemer
lay hidden. His girlfriend
sat outside, smoking,
wrapped in a blanket
of fine wool
to insulate herself
against ghosts. A phrase
heard in an empty room,
the oracle misheard,
interpreted by a
stupid man: *I trade gold
for wood.* So he had
lessened, wandering
alone by night to
stand naked among weeds
and rubbish in order
to greet the first
dog to climb the sky:
not Sirius but Procyon.

## 60

### 1

When he passed me, I
saw that his otherwise
nondescript coat had
two zipped-up slits in
the back, as if to make
allowance for wings.

### 2

Singing, yelling at the
old woman beside him,
he pushed a trolley
stacked with lengths
of thin copper pipe
across the road to the
labour club: at first, I
thought he had loaded
it with thunderbolts.

61

He criticised me
for the name I would
not reveal, hand I would
not offer, so much
more fastidious
than I had been in
youth when I took the
half-smoked cigarette
out of a street-
drinker's mouth to
light it in my own before
passing it back
(his hands too wobbly
to strike the match),
not out of compassion
but because I did
not give a fuck,
being numb as I was
when, with indifference
more shameful than
fear, I left the
old man to get beaten
up in the market: I
wondered afterwards
if I would have
intervened if either
he or his assailant had
been white.

62: *Vitriol*

She circulates the
ghostly substance
of money, for which
gold is an abandoned
god. Behind her,
the eagle and the
lion keep watch over
mercury and platinum,
phantoms of capital
generated by
the *Grundrisse*: the
creatures themselves
are split forms
of the griffins that
once guarded Apollo's
mines. (So I
found messages left
for myself in my old
aleatory texts,
had been my own oracle.)

63

1

I wished to read once again those incomprehensible stories of lives undone by a glance, a promise made before no significant company.

2

The prolonged slither and click of the beads dedicated to Green Tara (image of the Girl Prince): their coolness and the scent of sandalwood.

3

How could I not take it as some kind of omen when, one after the other, two small birds flew, or were tumbled by the sudden breeze, against my chest?

4

Mould grew upon the food not accepted: I remembered the drakaina too numb with alcohol to transmit, hiding the meal that had been carried to her.

5

Marius poured blond hair through the circular gateway in the tree trunk (eye socket through which I gazed): within the bower it appeared as coiling rays of light.

6

The fox no longer outside my office: it had given a sign of disinterest when I remarked that I must work by starlight in order to make love in the day.

7

Each attempt at heathen government defeated: we exist through wars that would have made Pound rock with laughter.

8

No history but the history of secret societies: a contract agreed before the puddles in the woods, the snake I rested my foot upon.

9

The ground dense with roots, standing proud of leaf dust, such poor soil: nature gives the sigils we use to glitterbomb the city.

10

Purposeful crow, I gaze through a tongue of flame at the feather you shed: the needle of the compass points toward the star-goddess.

Lightning Source UK Ltd.
Milton Keynes UK
03 March 2011

168562UK00001B/106/P

9 781905 700295